SMALL SALVATIONS

SMALL SALVATIONS

Patricia Dienstfrey

Kelsey St. Press   Berkeley 1987

*Grateful acknowledgment is made to the
Alameda County Artsfund for a grant
which made this book possible.*

*Book design by Robert Rosenwasser
Drawings by Kate Delos*

*PS3554.I355S6 1987 811'.54 87-14028
ISBN 0-932716-22-9*

I am grateful to Brenda Hillman, Frances Phillips and Rena Rosenwasser for their insights and comments.

To Ragdale Foundation I am thankful for grants in 1986 and 1987.

color akin to L *celare* to conceal—more at HELL.

hell OE *helan* to conceal, ON *hel* heathen realm of the dead,
Gk *kalyptein* to cover, Skt *śarana* screening, protecting

WICKED MOTHERS

I *GUESS THERE* is
in us a wicked
mother, that quick
majestic being who is basically
columnar and slowly descends
the downward
stairs. With a dark
line through her
from vagina to throat.
It's black. Sometimes

it's a poison we know
we drank in that infancy that's sleep
before memory, no different
from the womb.
            And remember.

It's green
and seen underwater as black
light in a glass tube.
At thirty and forty,
our shining deaths,
still and contained.

At other times
it's thin, wily, more
like the thing we use. Indestructible
as we bend to brush
our daughter's hair
and hold her arms steady
while she squirms herself
out of a sweater that's grown
too small.
        It's the old

conductor. Out of sight,
out of mind.
Now out of use. We've forgotten
as we've lost memories of ocean currents, roots

and words. As once a **wick** was
a dwelling place, dairy
or house; **vicus**, a net or noose,
basic meaning, to weave,
web; once akin to a corner
or to Old English
wik, bay, creek
and Old Norse **wikja**, to move,
turn aside;
compare weak.
In Middle English wick

plus -*ed* became contrary
to divine law,
              disgusting;
witch-like. Wicked
was used to describe witches'
potients and sabbath
flights, said by the Roman Church
authorities to cause
storms and deaths.
They massacred women
who witnessed for this power
and burned witches.

O mourned wisdom,
now archaic.
Yet it brushes us,
the early, partly

missing. Like the drowsing
air around a new baby, left alone
for the first time, nursed,
curled with her small head towards a corner
of her carrying bed.
Safe. The atmosphere

we walk through softly
and down the hall.
As if the hall
were a noon we've come to,
finding in ourselves
something new
is stirring.
        Content,

beyond ourselves, still
we continue
looking. Is there something
we've found,
or we're finding, or are
about to? Like someone else's
day on the beach—
a towel, a pair of glasses
        left behind?

TWO CORNERS

MY *MOTHER TURNED* two corners to come home. One turned her away from Hanover Street, the main street that brought her up the hill on the bus. The other turned her from Beacon Street onto the front walk of our yellow house.

That first time followed a snowstorm. The bus pulled away from the corner, the sound of chains in snow, and she appeared. She wore a fox collar, with the mouth clamped high on the tail, and a brown hat. The black veil she sometimes wore up, cloud-like, over the front of the hat, was down for the cold and formed a curve that was faithful to her face.

At the first corner she was a stranger. A lady wearing a brown coat and a hat with a thick veil. I remembered her from books. She walked with a light, quick step. She was on her way past our house.

By the time she had turned the second corner and said, "Good work," and started picking her way up the treacherous path, looking for the front door key in her purse, she had become younger. And I had become a wanderer in our yellow house and the lives of our family—as mother, father, daughter, soldier/son—in no particular order.

My father had come to the window of the upstairs bedroom and was looking down at the front walk. Light reflected off his glasses and beamed, one hard white line of focus, through the bare branches of the maple tree.

I loved my mother's brown coat and the fur pulled to the veil, her body sheathed, on the landing, like the spring shoot of a lily.

But I'd come unprepared. Her key was out and in the lock. She opened the door.

✦

I tend her memory like an acolyte her altar.

The air stirred, beaten in circles by heavy wings.
She went into the house and we begin again.

✤

She comes home with unvarying kindness, tireless when she appears on
Hanover Street ready to start. A woman with a patch of blue sky
over her head.

I'm resting, propped on my shovel, a somewhat flighty girl of twelve
who's pinned to the ground by a beam of light that's entered the top
of her skull and shot down her spine. An interjection into the story of
another, more original hunger—my father's, before my own.

I slam my shovel on the walk, my heart the heart of a soldier brought
to attention, proud the general's wife has arrived on his watch.

For a moment I'm enraged at the give of the metal shovel. Then fear
and bitterness mix, the way light makes orange when broken in a
prism.

Why can't I break anything?

✤

I'll never forgive myself. I let her by, just watched her pick her way
up the walk, in those little rubber boots she pulled over the toes of her
high heels in winter.

"Good work." In the veil, her face appeared worn. Like stone in a
garden. A heart-shaped piece fallen off a pedestal. A woman asleep in
a garden, her cheek on a bed of lilies-of-the-valley and violets.

Mom. Stop.

✤

It's winter and dark in the afternoons between the two darknesses of
night and morning. Home, I take on the role of ghost, the part
between. I put my hand out and become the yellow pistils in the roses

on my wallpaper and the diagonal-barred pattern of my parents'
sea-colored bedroom walls, and slip through.

A girl who knows colors as links to exiles she has no words for. And
looks into her parents' bureau drawers, like Narcissus into a
cosmology of fern-ringed ponds. In her father's, at the top, are
cufflinks, his doctor's key, a watch, a shoe horn.

In her mother's are two stacks of Irish linen handkerchiefs with
hand-whipped hems, notepaper, and a little pile of many-times-
laundered white cotton gloves.

✶

"Traitors," the man whispered, looking out the window at his wife and
daughter. He meant betrayers, but he spoke of state secrets.

He meant: "Those two are mine and they're whispering on the
corner. And why is *my* room silent?"

✶

What he can't hear them saying he calls seditious. In his heart he
assigns them to Hell's lowest circle. To frozen ground. To lie like
straws in ice with Dante's traitors to lords and country, whose tears
of repentance lock into visors over their eyes and mouths.

And reaches around for what's closest at hand. It's the little chair to
his wife's vanity table, which he slams on the carpet at the foot of
their high, white four-poster bed.

✶

"Two of them, just alike," he whispered, "two dark passages without
end." And continued on his way to get some work done around the
house, disgusted at the sight of the row of perfume bottles under his
wife's mirror.

I go back to the corner. To a place of continual erasure and shadowless walks and lawns. I call her, but I don't know her name. Margaret? My mouth opens. Ma'am?

The old names come back—Hanover, veil, home—to the sounds of shoveling and chains. Slowly they give way to shape and lend the first simple form to hearing, that waiting, walless cave.

And my father's home and looking out the window, his face in the branches. He's changed into the old clothes he wears to work around the house, the glint of light off his glasses an element of chance. And of the need for reassurance, for which he is up before dawn to hunt the answers to the secrets he calls codes. A man who is always on his way, like light to corners, to inhabit my bones—

When the woman turns in at the front of the house and heads up between the walls I've carved with my shovel. "Good work." The yellow house appears at the end of the walk and the key shines in my mother's glove. Her hand turns.

The dark edge widens. The white door draws to a line.

The circular beating of wings drains the air of colors. They all run out in their own directions. In all directions, like a wheel-shaped rainbow. Through the air, which is a sieve.

Windows open and close. Crocuses appear around the maple.

It's spring and summer in the yellow house, where we go to live a few more days of our lives. Until it's winter and the city's quiet under a fresh cover of snow and the streets are clear.

THE HOUSE BEHIND THE FIELD

IT'S *A HAUNT*, sweet
and full of authority,
oppressive as the lead
in my father's voice
that lay on my heart
when I played in the field, its murmur
reading the Bible.
The leather bookmark hung
down his knee like the tongue
of Everyman.
        Over time

The house became
a luminous mass, thick
               with family—
a net of passages
through which everyone passed
through everyone else
on his way toward the dream of innocence
I was closest to—
        The youngest

"Stoopie" my brother took
as his own, some time
in that sleep that's childhood
before memory. Probably
in the upstairs study with the lamp on
beside the globe—

That's where he brought his friends.
And I stood eye-level with open belts
and penises that smelled of paste
and rooms in other houses.
Not like my brother's. His
was soft as crushed velvet
and its dampness smelled of a flowerbed
in a shaded corner
of our backyard.
                    I took this

As a family secret,
                    into my mouth, mixed
with play and subjection
through kindergarten and first grade
and on to puberty.

This has been spoken of publicly
in the radiant civilization
of my mind, in traffic
no one sees. Not my father
and mother asleep
between their nightstands.

On his, his glasses
and candy. On hers a sewing basket,
knitting and a stack
of church women's magazines
she'll never get through—

The room I put behind me Sundays
at their end of the hall.
The door was closed, a stone rolled
over it like a tomb.
            It stayed

That way while I was in my brother's
room which faced east
and opened above the field
like a dandelion, unscattered, full
of light—

But when I was back
in my gray south,
with my bed and desk the sun
hadn't got around to
yet, it yawned
        and released

My father, unshaved,
in his bathrobe,
my mother on her way
to make breakfast.
            Her knock
on my door said,
Are you up? It's time
to get dressed.
Breakfast's eight.
Church's ten.

LET THE RASPBERRY JAM IN THE
CRYSTAL JAR STAND FOR IT

LET *THE RASPBERRY* jam in the crystal jar stand for it,
the spoon on the lace on the lazy susan.
Oranges, toast.
Everything was on

when our father read from the blood-soaked battles
of Old Testament history,
and we bowed our heads—
                    Something was missing.

Orangehood.
The whole fruit
in the first taste on our tongues.
Was it hunger the fullness

of every day fell off?
Our appetites, each with a morning
of its own?

Or was it our mother sitting under the clock
making seconds of toast?
                    She was the one

who brought things home
in grocery bags and smiled over them
on the threshold. Promising,

like a dove with an olive branch in her mouth,
but without a convenant
or rainbow—
A small woman. We hugged

her. Little Samsons, we strove
among ourselves to punish her. We listened
for her bones to snap.

But what we heard was something
like a music box
with the dancer on top

twirling in a clearing,
where sunlight was
breaking over treetops
onto her lifted face and skirt.
                    Then let mornings

and breakfast stand for it,
and everything on the lazy susan,
when we turned to what we wanted—
milk, eggs, salt—

And our mother
sat with the steam of a second cup of coffee
on her hair and face—

When the sunlight poured over the neighbors' fence
and onto the table
through the red velvet drapes,
we tasted *Butterhood, whole,*
                    a slick

flood of promise,
and were filled with hunger
in an undivided house.

ONE

SHE *LIVED IN* a country with one of everything in it—one
farm, one black cow, one red cow, one wild black horse.
One stone wall, one fence of every kind, each with or

Without its gate. There was so much of one of

Everything—one city with one shop of every
description—she lived in a perpetual state of the visiting
traveller passing scenes necessarily left behind.

Because one elm is coming into leaf. And one
car is drawing up to the curb, one with one family of
children jumping out, waving good-bye to one woman

Whose face is a blur in the car window
that is gray as a lake.

She lived in a country with one house of every kind, one
room with one lamp and one fear. The light of the lamp
covered her head like a cloche.

One night in a room that was cozy. One night in a room that
had no roof and one wall was missing. There was one long
hesitation, one refusal,

And one struggle. One death of a woman wearing white,
one man one dawn kneeling over her on the beach where the
country's long knife was pulled down the center

Of a woman who was just waking up. And there was one
division.

She looked for the woman everywhere in the morning in the
country where there was one waiting, one sleep, one dream
and one street of every description.

ELEMENTS OF THE GIFT

T HE *GIFT IS* for her and you ask for a box.

At first the gift looks lost in the box. But the precise geometry of the corners sets into relief the gift's more suggestive shape.

For instance, the sweater with the fake pearl and plastic bead yolk. First put in the box it looks slack. But it also looks exactly like itself.

It's angora, a little shopworn, taken out of the counter and put back too many times. Off-white, not dead-white like the box. And the little beads glitter.

The slack is made up with tissue. To give the papers more body filling in the corners, I separated the sheets— they came in groups of five— and wrapped the present in one at a time, using as many as it took to hold the gift, without crushing it, in the box.

Wrapping is necessary. The gift is all necessity in some form.

Among the elements of the gift are: order, the continual recreation of slowness, concealment.

After wrapping, the waiting begins. We wait. That's what we're doing now. Waiting and looking ahead to the opening.

Every opening is different. Every time, of course, the gift is different. Variety is one of its elements. But there is a constant—the expression of happiness we imagine on her face when she opens the box.

Her whole attitude of joy and astonishment over the open box.

I watch her hands untying the ribbon and finding the edges of the paper, her fingers sliding along the tissues, separating them. The angle she holds her head is important.

The tissue slows the opening and gives us time to see details and ask questions. Are her elbows far from her body? Does she rush? Why? What's in her?

I watch, a single-celled, divided creature propelled by hundreds of tiny processes. A ciliate life swimming towards her in the hope, it seems I was born with, of entering her soul.

Is she pale?

Might she stop and leave the gift unopened in the box? And stare at nothing. And choose nothing?

Keep in mind her desire to discover what it is you've given her this time, to unwrap the box, and pull the layers of tissue over the sides again.

Keep in mind the expression on her face the gift was chosen to reflect.

THE VEIL

WHAT *THE GIRL* saw was an excavation of the site of the feminine in the black hanging down. It permitted insight and concealed. It took on a feminine history that begins with the particular and goes back to beginnings. Like any object a woman has touched: needle, cup, iron.

Notepaper, carpet, field. An excavation, a surface suddenly lost. What then? There's more than appears in a chair! Wood, batting, thread, springs.

Overwhelmed, she avoided her mother's room. If she went in—she had to—she looked straight ahead and made up surfaces: white, smooth. A bathroom.

Horses, a tree. She didn't look at her mother or think "mother," "woman," and stopped anyone who said words that were about her: "Silver." Sshh.

She banged her shovel. She stuck to it like a soldier to his gun. Excavate. Sshh.

The face in the veil was indistinct. Kind. The air sighed. It moaned the moans of generations. Women's and children's eyes were clear. Their noses indistinct. Their mouths a series of coverings and uncoverings that filled with earth and emptied themselves in words. "Good." "Work."

Here was an opportunity. But there was too much to go through. More than a simple door. The key was caught in the veil. In generations of feminine history, in the net, a tree. Things. The richness was overwhelming. There was too much time.

Boredom took her by the throat. There was no time for mercy.

Damn, she should have killed him with the scissors, gone to the spot in his back when he was bending over to wind the clock. *She* could have rid their days of him and made it a safer world for generations of women and children crying to be free of the prison of his body, all waving guns.

Poor girl. Lost. Poor mother. Stop.

Sshh. "I don't think of my mother. There'll be no more house, or things that open. They will be opened, without more 'in' or 'out' or traps."

Any word was a trap. "Late." "Early." Sshh.

She'd come in in the middle, she thought. She'd planned to stay on top and not disappear. But she'd been caught on the corner of the walk to the front door of her own house. On a path she herself had cleared, the shovel in her hand part of her shadow.

And her mother was receding, her face a veil over something that was sweet and vague.

And whole and sticky in the girl's mind as a candy apple at the county fair, where skin had been a temptation behind a tent flap. She'd heard sighs and had fallen asleep, her cheek on the canvas in the lights of the ferris wheel.

Love takes a woman's skin. It lifts her flesh and takes it from her. Stop. Don't look.

The girl stood with her eyes ahead. She developed a glance that stopped her mother cold and anyone who was the girl's friend necessarily ignored. And her father sent her upstairs for and told her to close her door.

She let herself be touched. She couldn't be alone. Stop. Sshh. She touched, because she couldn't help notice things were lovely. She reached out.

Into the thing. She was touched where there was no surface. Where she opened, she

Didn't stop. No matter which way she turned her hand was out. A painter's brush dripping with pigment. Color. Sshh.

THE VISIT

O *MY MOTHER* has gone
and she will never come again.

Now my doorway will always be empty
of her body and arrival.
I'll never prepare the way

I used to when she was coming,

when I got down on my hands and knees and scrubbed —

As I saw her do when I was young.
How I hated her when she was down there

in the dust, her hands
in dirty water. *My Mother!*

*Gone over to the enemy
in camouflage!*

But then I got back into corners and under beds.

I vacuumed, mopped, polished

until she was on my stairs and the bell rang.
This is how she entered —

Her veil up
like a visor —

She carried a black leather
purse with compartments
she set on her chair like a model house.

Taking her gloves off, finger by finger,
she looked around
as if at nothing—

As if my walls were glass.

She counted torn hems, missing buttons,
unpaired socks.

One by one things I'd neglected
she held up like crystals
on a chandelier she'd washed

and was reassembling.
My heart, too. She tested,

her fingers light
as the powder she spilled
on her dressing table runner, smooth

as the pink satin cushion I wasn't
to touch, but went to
in the dark when she wasn't there, *it seemed*

so like myself
among the other cushions

Now she's gone. And this emptiness
that's terror is more

than mine. I cry for myself,
my house, my city—

For what we'll waste
and leave to die.

NOW WHO WILL NOTICE?

But this morning I heard bells.

I was going over a stain in the sink
so impossible to get rid of, I thought
"My heart!"

I whispered it.

The spot opened
like a funnel—

"Mother!" I called, "come and visit me!"

The kitchen roof tilted,
a steeple, and cast

a sparkling air
like salt from a cellar.

The bell peeled the dark sound
of its own metal
through fields that had replaced the stairs.

The grass lay green, bent
by wind, but also under its own weight

like grain at the end of summer—

She was in my door, dusty and travel-worn.

More than the meeting
of our lips, the scent
of her *Fleurs des Alpes* facepowder

proved she was within
reach. "Please come in,"

I said, "I was calling you."

I rested my head on her lap while she stroked my hair

and everything we'd cleaned and saved, or torn
into scraps to use another way, opened

And called *MY ORDER—*

And all walls and doors were glass
reflections of

her NAMES, which the air repeated,

resonant on my face.

Small Salvations is a limited edition
of seven-hundred and fifty copies;
images by Kate Delos,
fifty hand-colored by the artist, numbered &
signed by the author.
Printed by Wesley B. Tanner on
a Miller Simplex press.
Typeset in Goudy Light by Mackenzie-Harris.
Mohawk Superfine text paper.
Gainsborough cover.
Book design by Robert Rosenwasser.

Kelsey St. Press   August 1987